# Its Shadow Rakes the Grass

# Its Shadow Rakes the Grass

Poems by

Bill Christophersen

© 2023 Bill Christophersen. All rights reserved.
This material may not be reproduced in any form, published,
reprinted, recorded, performed, broadcast,
rewritten or redistributed without
the explicit permission of Bill Christophersen.
All such actions are strictly prohibited by law.

Cover design by Shay Culligan
Cover image by Devesh Sangwan
Author photo by Alain Berger

ISBN: 978-1-63980-344-6

Kelsay Books
502 South 1040 East, A-119
American Fork, Utah 84003
Kelsaybooks.com

"My shadow sticks to the trees where gibbons scream."
—Tu Fu, "To My Younger Brother"

# Acknowledgments

The following poems have been previously published as indicated:

*Apalachee Review:* "Nature 1, Nurture 0"
*Comstock Review:* "Shadow"
*Hanging Loose:* "Fridge," "Limbo of Lost Gloves," "Rainstorm," "The Human Balcony"
*Mojave River Review:* "Sin-Eater"
*Rattle:* "Hole"
*Right Hand Pointing:* "Pioneering the New Frontier"
*Rhino:* "Some Personas"
*Sierra Nevada Review:* "One Remove"
*Tampa Review:* "Autumn Haiku," "Country Road, Hamilton County," "Semblance," "The New Self"
*Yale Review:* "Central Park: December," "Heretics"

# Contents

Semblance                                          13

## Hole

Hole                                               17
Declension                                         21

## The Cypress' Knees

The New Self                                       25
Cyclical                                           26
Southern Exposure                                  27
Oktibbeha Spring                                   35
Alligator                                          36
The Cypress' Knees                                 37
One Remove                                         38
Rainstorm                                          40
Outage                                             41
Nature 1, Nurture 0                                42
Ain't Like That                                    43
Heretics                                           45
Country Road, Hamilton County                      46
Central Park: December                             47

## Valley of the Shadow

Generational Thing                                 51
Off-White Christmas                                52
Ativan                                             54
Baptist Memorial Hospital                          55
Winter Sonnet                                      56
Funky Umbrella                                     57

## Government Cheese

| | |
|---|---|
| Government Cheese | 61 |
| U.S. 80 West, with the Barnstormers | 62 |
| Trad Dance | 65 |
| Exploding Toads? | 67 |
| Popular Cetology | 69 |
| "Chess Robot Grabs and Breaks Boy's Finger" | 71 |
| Thank You for Your Patience | 72 |
| Complimentary Tool | 73 |
| Reading the News Online | 74 |
| To the Kansas Board of Education | 75 |
| Donut Shop | 76 |
| Pioneering the New Frontier | 77 |

## Shadow

| | |
|---|---|
| Riverside Park: September | 81 |
| Blood Moon | 82 |
| Sin-Eater | 83 |
| Whodunit | 84 |
| Persona Non Grata | 85 |
| Sagaponack | 86 |
| From between Parked Cars | 87 |
| Lost Edge | 88 |
| Math for Poets | 89 |
| Tumbleweed Mischief | 91 |
| Phatic | 92 |
| "Dig Deep!" | 93 |
| Fridge | 94 |
| Shard | 95 |
| Van Cortlandt Park: November | 96 |
| Thanksgiving, 2016 | 97 |

Limbo of Lost Gloves (A Double Feature)     99
Some Personas                                100
What She Notices                             101
Autumn Haiku                                 102
Cold Comfort                                 103
Health Salad                                 104
Chestnuts, Roasting                          105
The Human Balcony                            106
Shadow                                       107

*About the Author*                           109

# Semblance

You're crossing the avenue when
you're struck
by the shadow of a veering
truck. You're
untouched—perfectly okay.
But you'll
live in the shadow of that
shadow play.

Hole

# Hole

When the toddler disappeared (the septic tank's
countersunk manhole cover not quite centered
and so become a revolving door), the May
sun was drying the grass of the bed-and-breakfast's
manicured front lawn. A gardener
was coaxing a power mower up the property's
street-side incline, one hand on the throttle,
the other on the driving wheel's black dish.

When the father disappeared (down the same hole,
self-preservation trumped by something else
more limbic still, some gut-level imperative
or sense that hell had got him by the balls,
no matter how he played it), the mother, alone
and shaking, screamed with her whole body.
The gardener jammed the stick in park and hove
his lumbering, sweating self from the metal seat.

Then the mother disappeared (belayed
by the gardener's sausage fingers round her ankles,
arms flailing the stinking darkness; flailing
and groping, the acrid stench suffocating
as her terror—the epiphany that life,
into which we bring these ones we love,
can snatch them by the toe and eat them whole;
can leach their little hides, do what we will).

Then the child reappeared (hauled up bodily,
the mother, arms extended like a midwife's,
seizing it in midair from the father,
who, plunging deep, had gone to work, feeling
past turds till hand touched skull, then tugged
the curled-up infant from the pissy muck
and raised it above his head, a living trophy—
delivered to its mother, then babe and mom delivered

by the puffing gardener, whose yells of "Help! Baby!"
brought a passing mom-and-stroller, hence clean
water, disinfectant wipes, cell phone and the steady
voice required to summon 911).
Below, the father, treading bilious sludge,
barked knuckles on cement, then struck a rung—
egress from that twilight zone of filth;
chimney to pure light, sun-drenched salvation.

And so the father reappeared (climbing
out of deeper shit than I or anyone
I know has ever been encompassed by.
One doesn't think, they say, at times like this;
one reacts. One thinks all sorts of things: How deep?
Well? Cesspool? Caustic chemicals? Will I
land on him? Break his back? My back? Is he
dead already? Am I committing suicide?

The ambulance arrived in a minute-thirty.
Son and father had stomachs pumped, got meds,
caught colds, got better. All three wake up screaming
more often than most of us. The parents shower
way more than they need to. The two-year-old
climbs the walls at the mention of bath time but
otherwise is doing fine. Turns out babies
hold their breath instinctively under water.

*

One wants the tale to end there, and perhaps
it does, a centerpiece of family lore, a
miracle of love, bravery, a special
dispensation all three share going forward.

But perhaps the enormity of the episode,
like a dark star, warps the space around it,
and the debt of love incurred toward the father
smothers the wife, and later the child, in guilt.

Perhaps the father, a dozen or more years later,
watching his teenage son do reckless things,
thinks, "What right's he got to pull this kind
of shit on me?" Or, seething at the wife's
obiter dicta and bickering retorts,
thinks, "Why was it up to me to take the plunge?
Was my life more expendable than yours?"
Perhaps the boy, unable at last to abide

the horror of that day, its happy ending
notwithstanding, loses the knack for trust,
without which nothing much is ever ventured,
fought for, wrestled with, maintained in spite
of obstacles? Perhaps no foothold ever
fully persuades; no morning sun on green
lawn but signifies some nightmare's mise-
en-scene; no darkness seems negotiable.

*

A miracle is deceptive. Isolated,
it can make all history seem foreordained,
as if the jeweled part stands for the whole
bloody mess, that far less scintillating
prospect. There's the chance, of course, that life's
a latticework, a series of intersecting
miracles or miracle plays whose characters
appear/disappear within the larger structure,

a glimpse of which we're occasionally afforded:
no clockwork universe but one ably directed
by the playwright himself, who, understandably
perhaps, bends over backward to retain
his privacy, anonymity, invisibility,
though peering, now and then, from a wing to nod
or appearing, like Alfred Hitchcock, in a cameo—
as grandfather, gardener, *deus ex machina*.

A tempting proposition, this invisible
script, this hidden teleology
in which each of us plays an unwitting part.
But over and against it is the hole—
unspeakable; mephitic; defiling;
predatory, one almost wants to say;
lying there beneath resplendent grass
on which young couples and their babies play.

# Declension

Ground, matted with leaves. *Color?* Salmon,
wine, raw umber, dirty yellow. *Texture?*
Splattered. Imbricated. *Yeah? So?* No
dice. It stops right there. *Beyond "there" being . . . ?*
Romance. The place where we talk about ourselves
in terms of trees, seasons. Where the buck-naked
pear is my dead father, my decrepit mother, me
in a couple decades, my skinny limbs flayed
of maculate skin, no longer itching. *An
abstract canvas?* Yup. Colors laid on with a
palette knife, a rag, a pop-stick, resembling
nothing. *Nothing at all? Really?* But
whole, you know? Elaborate—a world.

# The Cypress' Knees

# The New Self

Begin again? And in the face of so
much whiteness, like a gauntlet, thrown down?
Pick up a handful. Now the blight's your own.
Fingers ache, stop working. Bare hands grow
numb. Eventually, the season's hold
unclenches. Blenched members flush and sting
back to life. (Cue the crocuses.) The weathering
isn't guaranteed, though. Here's a cold
numbs the spirit as it does the skin;
makes a dead branch of the broken will;
freezes every prospect fast, until
a kind of cabin fever settles in,
the old self despising itself, that monkey's paw. . . .
The new? Whatever's lucid, come the thaw.

# Cyclical

You notice it in the very trough of winter:
Daylight in January perseveres
a little longer than it did at Christmas.
And though the plane trees' noonday shadows score
the bike path in the park and shriveled clumps
of bittersweet wizen alongside the expressway,
mocking October's road show the way the stripped
chassis of a Mustang rusting in the woods
behind a Mississippi trailer park derides
some old-timer's dream of open roads,
still, the sense of slow amelioration,
of incremental hope, energizes
something in the brain that's eager to believe
rejuvenation, like the highway, goes on forever.

# Southern Exposure

The TV's on. The Lunesta butterfly's bioluminescent
wings sprinkle sleep on stressed suburbanites, chill now
atop a rumpled comforter. . . . I switch the channel,
look for a movie but get distracted by my surroundings:
Mom's new home in rural Mississippi. A ranch house
at the corner of a subdivision, it faces woods on one side
and an African American church and grounds behind.
It's a serene neighborhood (once you get used to the
year-round routine of tornado watches and warnings).
Mom turns in early, so I've stretched out in the recliner.
TV aside, it's quiet. Earlier, fighter jets doing aerial
maneuvers in the skies above Columbus Air Force Base
kept things humming, but at night . . . What a place
to fetch up after living in New York! This morning, I
took a walk past railroad tracks, cotton fields. The ghosts
of Chaney, Schwerner and Goodman shimmered amid
the heat vectors. . . . I'd hitchhiked brashly through most
of the continental United States after college in '71,
but had avoided the Deep South. Decades later, I still
wasn't sure the next pickup with the inevitable gun rack
wouldn't suss me out for a damn Yankee and
run me off the road. The walk was uneventful. Was
the New South cutting me some slack or just lulling me
into complacence? The Lunesta ad pops up again—
the third time in forty-five minutes.

*

Mississippi *is* alien: crawfish turrets on the asphalt's
sandy shoulder; saw palmettos—holdouts, surely, from
the Pleistocene era—bristling along the woods' edge;
snakes; state troopers whose mirror shades hide eyes that
might not see things my way; fire ants (a nursing-home
invalid fell asleep eating birthday cake and was swarmed
by an army of them coming through an open window;

their nests, I've noticed, infest our yard). On the other hand,
I've been told the state holds several good surprises:
an Irish music scene in Jackson; 150-year-old architecture
in Oxford; cypress swamps; Faulkner's house, open to the
public; a thousand-year-old site where pre-Columbian
mound-builders lived; the Jimmie Rodgers Museum.

\*

After eight minutes of commercials, the opening credits
roll for—I'll be damned!—*In the Heat of the Night*,
a 1967 film set in small-town Mississippi. The cast
features Sidney Poitier and Rod Steiger, both leaning into
their roles. Steiger plays a volcanic sheriff who arrests
Poitier's character for murder, only to learn he is a homicide
detective from up north—Philadelphia. The white cop
winds up soliciting the black cop's expertise to solve
the murder case he and his men are bungling. It's a taut
film; the scene of grudging racial reconciliation it ends with
feels uncontrived, unsentimental. But who can forget
the "slap heard round the world"—the Poitier character's
response to a bigot who gives him the back of his hand?

\*

The Jimmie Rodgers Museum in Meridian is a shiny boxcar
full of predictable memorabilia—the Singing Brakeman's
flat-top Martin guitar (his name all mother-of-pearled along
the frets, the instrument kept in a temperature- and humidity-
controlled safe), various framed LP album covers featuring
his railroad-capped phiz and thumbs-up pose—and some
random props (the water keg he used while on the job, a pair
of fancy cowboy boots that, presumably, belonged to him).

Under glass are handbills advertising the Blue Yodeler's coming appearance at one venue or another, photos of his family's home and the like. A fan-friendly but forgettable spot but for the last item in the case: a two-page handwritten letter from Jimmie to his mom, dated a couple of weeks before his death from TB. In it the consumptive says he's doing better, feeling good in fact, and looking forward, "as always, to seeing his best girl again real soon."

\*

I'm raking leaves in the yard, scooping them into plastic bags. Beyond the fence I see Mom's neighbor, whose house sports a confederate flag. I stop to ask him about the trash-collection schedule for the neighborhood and test the social waters. He says Friday mornings. I say I'm down from New York helping care for Mom. He says that's nice, it's good for a son to pitch in when the folks get old. Says he wishes he had done more for his folks in their later years, but he and his dad kept getting their wires crossed. *(Not a Snopes, evidently.)* He says it's a good area—just elevated enough to be above the flood plain. But he could do without the nigg-ras down the block, whose teenage son works on his car, Sundays, to the basslines of "a goddamn suitcase-size boom box."

\*

Then again, in a Starkville mall I watch a sixtyish white man strike up a conversation with the black serviceman at the next table in the food court. It's mostly small talk. But it doesn't have to happen. I've seen the same thing at the airport, though that might have been flying jitters

playing out. Churches, it seems plain, self-segregate.
School kids at lunch, I'm told, caucus in racial groups.
Bottom line: *I can't read the bottom line here.*

                      \*

My sister, Mom and I get up early, take a morning drive
to the Noxubee Refuge, where a long boardwalk lets you
all but walk on water. It's bright, and although spring
hasn't made any major moves yet, a snake of some kind
is splayed across the branches of a shrub, motionless
—a dead battery accessing solar power. Birds are busy,
their shards of color prinking the woody drab. Ancient
cypresses all but shame you outright for turning up here
in your manufactured clothes and mortal coil.

                      \*

As the season heats up, Mom struggles to stay warm.
Struggles for words. She wants more from me than
small talk, but doesn't remember narrative threads
well enough to converse much. We talk about family,
repeat ourselves hourly, and do this every day. TV
covers the silences between meals. I have my work—
the online editing that keeps me solvent, the research
I'm doing on Faulkner's Yoknapatawpha tales. I retreat
into the one when the other lets me come up for air.
Not that I don't make time for crossword puzzles, rides,
backyard birdwatching—things we can still do together.
They matter. They are catalysts. Mom remembers odd
details and sometimes figures out unlikely crossword
clues ("rani," "ideate," "evert"—are you kidding me!).
But she gets frustrated a lot. So do I. I sometimes

despair of keeping up my end of what has begun to feel
like prefab patter, talk for talk's sake. The Mom
I know and love is vanishing in plain sight.

*

It's Sunday afternoon, and the gospel singing in the
ramshackle church behind the house has segued to
less-soothing sounds. The youth fellowship plays
basketball, wiffle ball and whatnot on the tarmac
driveway. Reminds me of how, growing up, I'd
toss a ball against the wall of my building, annoying
elderly residents. But I'm feeling short-fused, and
Mom is obsessing about it, so I take a trip around
the corner to speak a few well-considered (I hope)
words to the minister. He proves to be a genial guy,
formerly a chaplain at Fort Eustis Army Base in
Newport News. We chat a bit. Virginia, he agrees,
is the South but not the Deep South, though he's
not inclined to make too much of the difference.
I like the man and can't bring myself to broach the
reason I've stopped by. I turn to leave, and as we
shake hands, he says, "I'll tell the guys to keep it
down. Any time they get on your nerves, give me
a buzz and I'll remind them that we're all part of a
larger community and need to keep that in mind."
*Whew! Talk about a gospel in a nutshell. . . .*
I return, chastened, to the house, where Mom has
the TV's volume cranked almost to one hundred.

*

*It's 1958, and I'm getting ready for school. The
morning news is on, and a reporter says that in
rural Mississippi, a Negro teenager was found dead,
hung upside down from a tree. He'd been beaten
with chains; the letters KKK had been carved in his
chest. My mother stops me on my way out the door:
"Whoa! You've got your sweater on backwards!"*

\*

We take a day trip to the Delta—get out of the house,
reconnect, see the state, maybe visit bluesman Robert
Johnson's grave, if we can find it. That's my thing.
Nobody else knows who the man is, what he was
known for. The noonday temperature is a hundred.
We stop in the Delta town of Greenwood, most of
whose stores are boarded-up. A thin black man
standing in a doorway is the only person visible
on Main Street. I enter a corner general store, where
half a dozen men are drinking ice teas, say I'm
looking for Robert Johnson's gravesite. *(Crickets.)*
At last, a man on a stool says, "Robert *who?*"
"Johnson. Blues guitarist. Sold his soul, they say,
back there at the crossroads . . ." The silence metastasizes.
Maybe they're right: *What the hell am I doing here?*

\*

It's late—2 a.m.? 2:30? I've been asleep and
awakened to silence and a snowy screen. I've been
dreaming about bad weather on Long Island. . . .
And now I remember the time that Mom and I
went to see about a nursing home for Grandma. . . .

*We take a train, then a bus, then walk a mile down
a dirt road. Just before it dead-ends at an airfield, we
come to the advertised address—a three-story, gray-
shingled house with five cadavers in rocking chairs
on the porch. Plane exhaust hangs in the humid air.
No one rocks or speaks. Inside, specked flypaper
hangs in amber spirals. Big spider in the sink.
No attendants visible. Who, my mother says,
would commit an aged parent to a place like this?*

\*

My sister stops by. She'd been doing yardwork in the
brush by the creek at the far end of her property when
she raked up a cottonmouth. They will bite and bite
again—give no quarter. She hadn't been bit. She had
called the zoo, and they'd sent a man in hip boots with
a forked stick and croker sack. He'd found the snake,
trapped and removed it—a pregnant female, as it
turned out, and therefore sluggish. . . . Cottonmouths
will rear up from water and strike you in your row boat.
They'll strike at bare feet dangling from a dock. . . .
Well, my sister says, I had my rake.

\*

It's 4:35—I've stayed up crazy late, a bad habit I've
slipped into down here. Again, the Lunesta butterfly
flutters across the screen, sprinkling blue-green sleep
on luckier souls than I. Mom will be up in an hour.
I turn off the TV and stagger to my room. What's to
become of this 98-year-old woman whose days are
winding down in this house behind which hawks and

eagles ride the thermals, of an afternoon, looking for
whatever skittering snack presents itself?

*

And *Mississippi?* How to come to terms with a place
whose past, says Faulkner, isn't even past—and whose
present I can't seem to integrate? A place whose
racial tensions are, well, my own? Whose Dollar Stores,
catfish farms, churches, antebellum mansions, cypress
swamps and roadhouses coexist in surreal suspension?
Whose flagship novelist's prose is as unkempt—and
mesmerizing—as the kudzu-entrammeled woods that
abut state roads? Whose native inhabitants' monumental
mounds extrude behind the New South's industrial parks?

# Oktibbeha Spring

Redbuds, dogwoods, coral
azaleas shaking loose . . .
The cane brake's decked in
new threads, huh? Old trees
meshed in kudzu, Virginia
creeper, a dusting of pale
yellow, off-white, red up top . . .
Wisteria's holding back:
mostly bare branches, a
touch of bronze, some
wispy stuff there in the
thick. . . . The pines—well,
they're pines, you know, the
Seminoles of the vegetable
kingdom, hang in there don't
matter what you throw at 'em. . . .
But, hooray, you gotta like that
lemon-lime piping 'round the edges!

# Alligator

Submerged, motionless,
in among the cypress' knees:
a log with nostrils.

# The Cypress' Knees

Resembling amputated
limbs, they issue from
the tree's root system,
protruding upward,
two or three feet
above swamp water.
Stabilizers? Aerobic
organs? A gambit
akin to the earthen
buttes made by
pre-Columbian
mound-builders?
(In a flood plain,
elevation isn't just
a warrior's edge.)
Is this how a tree
avoids drowning,
being swept away?
Surely these middle
fingers raised against
the elements embody
survival, never mind
the buzzards roosting
in the upper branches.

# One Remove

We stroll the wooden walkway at
the Noxubee Refuge, a foot above
cedar-tinged water, the bald-cypress
trunks and knees protruding. Orange
lichen ignites the underside of a
downed limb half swallowed
by muck and silt. A willow
arcs overhead. Beyond the
lake, in front of which we
pause for snapshots (Mom
cold despite the Norwegian
pullover), cormorants roost
in a bare stand of tupelo.

\*

Storks wade the shallows where
minnows flit. It's
March: no insects yet, a
mercy in the charcoal-filtered
sunshine. On a spit of land
a snapper, neck extended,
grapples an extruded root, the
stegosaurian profile sharp
against the ashen trunk. It
won't be long: April's
green machine, ducklings
moonwalking on water, the
snapper's jaws pulverizing.

\*

When the hip breaks, it
breaks in four places. We
hang on the surgeon's report,

chat up the physical therapists, rue
the callous transport aides, divide
the remnants of nibbled meals. Sweet
smells slip through the window in the
rehab unit until the sky goes green and
a code gray fills the corridor with
hospital beds, IV trees, piped pajamas.

    \*

Waves of pain segue to the
sound of memory flushing. It's
summer—a riot of leaves, roman-
candling of spores. No tiny
thing but has its day in the
sun, buzzes its signature buzz.
Old tissue mends. Old bones
bear up. Next season's
traumas gestate in the Gulf.

    \*

Back home, the New
York skyline rises, a
Plexiglas barrier reef, an
iridescent breastwork.

# Rainstorm

Purple clouds, hailstones
like slung ball bearings. The torn
skirts of umbrellas.

The rain ends. North on
Amsterdam, new green glistens
above traffic cones.

Black rainwater runs
a red light. Gypsy cabs hiss
past, honking for fares.

Steam rises from wet
asphalt in the neighborhood
known as Hell's Kitchen.

The humidity
intensifies. Hot air squats
like a double chin.

Another downpour:
Con Ed repairman cursing
in his galoshes.

# Outage

The Midtown Direct to Dover slows, then stalls
in a tract of marsh, where a sedulous wind
bends man-dwarfing phragmites, moves upon
the scummy water. Minutes from Penn Station
and we're out of our depth; power lost; stuck
in swamp where a half-digested shopping cart's
remaining wheel protrudes above the muck.
The roadbed bears us up, lets us be
tourists in this zone where ribbon snakes
and muskrats have outflanked us. Suburbia's
a foreign land—pale, inconsequential
as Manhattan's scumbled spires to these algae
that go on subdividing as the train,
its reckoning deferred, lurches into motion.

# Nature 1, Nurture 0

Goshawk? Falcon? No one is quite sure
here on College Walk, where last night's snow
is being plowed in head-high mounds and just
beyond, on a lime tree's lowest bough,
a brindled raptor eviscerates a pigeon,
pinning the carcass to the branch with one
set of talons while seeing to its perch
with the other. It's messy. Pigeon feathers
flutter on the breeze. Clots of flesh,
gouts of blood maculate the drifts.
Two dozen, maybe thirty passers-by—
undergrads, grads, adjuncts, faculty—
stop and stare. It's what the academic
community can't parse; has no words for.

# Ain't Like That

Kid, I'm proud of you! "Special Recognition:
Westchester Regional High School Science Fair,
'A Numerical Analysis of Intergenerational
Genetic Anomalies in *Drosophila*'"—If you don't
mind my askin', What the hell does that mean, huh?
Never mind. They were impressed, and so am I. And
I'm not just sayin' that 'cause those godawful jars
of fruit flies and three-month-old banana mash are
finally gone from the garage, jeez, what a stink.
When that cloud of no-see-'ems—I mean, what's
gauze to a fruit fly, right?—would swirl around my
head in the morning, I felt like one of those human
wrecks Don Martin used to draw in MAD. But
here's the thing: You're almost 18, you're gonna be
steppin' out into a world that looks like it's
always looked but isn't. A world that's
bright and sunny and full of sparrows, birds
that would kill you in your tracks if they were
a little bigger. No, really. I'm serious. You
took bio, you know the goddamn things are
descended from dinosaurs. They're reptiles in cammies,
snakes that go "tweet." When they hop over, give you that
sidelong glance, they're thinkin' they'd like to have your
eyeball for breakfast, though they'll settle for a couple of
crumbs from your toasted roll. Which by the way I don't
know how you eat with all that butter, you're askin' for a
coronary at 17.               You ever seen sparrows fight?
I watched a pair once, fightin' like kamikazes in the
air above Tremont Avenue in the Bronx. Tumbled
to the asphalt near a sewer, pecking, pecking, then
onto the grating and down the sewer, mud-wrestling
like Komodo dragons in the sludge. Finally the loser

escaped, the other one right on his tail, and the fight
continued down Belmont. I was young, like you.
It was early Sunday morning. I was thinking in, like,
Walt Disney animation frames—Uncle Remus talking to
the bluebirds, the Drifters' "Under the Boardwalk," my
girlfriend's legs glazed in Coppertone—that was before
they had the sunscreen factor on the packaging because
back then everyone thought the sun was good for you, like
you're some kind of tropical rubber plant, you know?
I'm just trying to tell you: *It ain't like that.*

# Heretics

The 4:10 local to Ronkonkoma
pulls in late and on the wrong track. I run
from 17 to 13, my eczema
flaring as it does when dog-day sun
and humidity combine to make my pants
legs stick to my perspiring skin.
Damn! I itch as if a horde of ants
were swarming me. My antihistamine's
worn off; no salve; too early for the evening
pill; blood specks one sleeve below the elbow. . . .
My doctor, a wry bastard, has this thing
he says whenever I complain: "I know. . . .
Nature has a million ways to break
us. . . . We're tied, like heretics, to her stake."

# Country Road, Hamilton County

We walk and play "I spy": fiddlehead
ferns; goldenrod; lupine; joe-pye weed;
a cranberry bog, the berries not yet red. . . .
The foliage has just begun to bleed.
A tropical storm's been through—the final wheeze
of a hurricane that came apart in gusts
but managed, nonetheless, to take down trees
and wash out roads and bridges. You can't trust
September. A felled pine's scraggly bole
protrudes above our heads—grotesque retort
to summer's lush and breezy protocols
that otherwise had mesmerized. Our sport
flags. But only for the time it takes to spy
this hovering, iridescent dragonfly.

# Central Park: December

Unfazed by fall's raw-
and burnt-sienna gouache:
willow's green fountain.


Mud puddle: pond scum,
half-submerged leaves, pigeon tracks,
wobbling skyscrapers.


A gale cleaves trees, boughs.
Two long-tailed claims adjustors
pick through the wreckage.


Bare circuitry of
oak, elm. How long before the
maple blows a fuse?


So cold the muzzled
Doberman's nostrils smoke. The
locust's harrowed bark.


A warm front melts the
hoarfrost on the tennis courts—
autumn's backhand smash.


Beside the lake, a
tossed pop-stick crawling with ants;
Manhattan Island.

# Valley of the Shadow

# Generational Thing

She couldn't get the hang of a microwave.
Put sweet potatoes in for forty minutes—
the time it would have taken on the stove.
Scratch one microwave. . . .
I bought a new one, explaining, etc.
The dryer taking too much time to
dry the morning wash, she grabbed
a bunch of damp T-shirts, socks, a rubber
glove, and threw them in. With
the predictable result: cottons charred,
rubber glove melted, wall scorched. The kitchen
stank for weeks, aerosol notwithstanding.
With much misgiving, I anted up and
bought one more, the simplest model on the market:
safety features, a color-coded set of buttons.
She thought she'd warm a jar of peaches, metal
lid and all. It exploded like a bottle rocket.

Her thoughts would wander back to how *her* mom
made scones on a wood-burning stove, flipping them
with her fingers, the timing instinctual, propping
the baked triangles, apex to nubby apex,
aslant each other to "brown the hypotenuse."

# Off-White Christmas

Out the window at dawn: frost and
a deer harassed by dogs, one haunch
mangled when it leapt the neighbor's
eight-foot hedgerow, which conceals
a cyclone fence. Mom, already up,
has pulled the tree down for the
second time in four days, convinced
Christmas has come and gone. Which,
hey, you might as well say it has. I
free the tree from the stand, drag it down
the driveway and pitch it, damned if I'm
going to set it up and trim it yet again. I'm
sweeping up as the deputy sheriff arrives
to put the deer down: *Poomph! Poomph!* What's
next, eh? That's when I spot the improvised
dining table centerpiece, a rectangular
Styrofoam base about 8 by 12 by 1,
to which are affixed a dozen or so
decomposing insect specimens on pins,
their faded labels like miniature scarves,
protruding from a skein of cobwebs.
As it comes into focus, I remember
seeing it in a pile of boxes in the garage—
something the niece did for a junior-
high-school science project once
upon a time. It sits atop Mom's hand-sewn
red-and-green satin pillow.

                              I'm no more
sentimental than the next guy, but
in my hand are the pieces of a
favorite ornament, a grandmother's
gift, the grandmother gone half a
century now, her 98-year-old daughter—
my mother, who tutored me in algebra
and talked me through a rough eleventh year—
smiling like a tot under mistletoe.

# Ativan

The drug to calm her down numbed her legs,
so we carried her into the house, into bed.
I hunkered in a chair to keep watch—
she was an accident waiting to happen.

We carried her into bed. But then
she needed to get up.
She was an accident waiting to happen.
I got one arm around her waist,

since she needed to get up,
but despite my help, she fell.
My arm was around her waist, but
she fell in all directions.

Despite my help, she fell
and hit her head on the table.
She fell in all directions at once.
This happened four more times.

She hit her head on one thing and another.
I was a lousy practical nurse.
This happened four more times that night.
After the second time, I started praying.

*Help her, dammit! Make me a better nurse!*
Mom's Australian shepherd trundled in to stare.
After the second fall, I started praying.
She fell three more times.

Each time, the dog came in to stare. . . .
The sedative had numbed Mom's legs.
The nightstand, the sink, the bedstead—
she was several accidents. They all happened.

# Baptist Memorial Hospital

The phone rings in the Soiled Utility room
and keeps on ringing. Down the corridor
an orderly disappears behind a door.
IV trees, their crimson fruit in bloom,
line one wall: Half a dozen or more,
pouches gravid with the stuff of life,
await those who have undergone the knife.
Green-scrubbed tech staff waltz them off the floor.
Most patients here recuperate. But some
are beyond help; will never be made whole.
In this, their Ellis Island of the soul,
they sweat out the preliminaries, dumb
with fear; or, blinking memories of strife,
dream the American Dream of an afterlife.

# Winter Sonnet

*for Isabel Christophersen, 1914–2013*


Olive, umber, brown, gray . . . Once more,
November's cubist palette, trotted out—
this time without much fanfare, yet a rout
of everything the year had bargained for:
Technicolor panoramas scorched,
grasses desiccated; branches rent;
foliage in tatters—autumn's tent
struck; gaunt limbs menacing the porch. . . .

My mother's is the porch I have in mind.
She contemplated wintertime with dread.
The last—her 99$^{th}$—robbed her blind:
broke her bones, then got inside her head
and scattered what it found there to the wind.
She died today, whom life had left for dead.

# Funky Umbrella

When I was twelve, my mother's
mother—a staunch Christian all
her life but widowed, senile and
increasingly anxious in her large,
empty house—committed suicide.
Mom, fearing the act doomed her for
eternity, began crying one night as we
walked home from the grocer's. Taking
the bag, I told her God would never
confuse an old person's desperation
with the ordinary kind of suicide.
I didn't yet know that every suicide
is an act of desperation; hadn't yet
come to suspect that eternity is
where we live, that hell doesn't
wait to have at us. My homily
must have pained as much as it
comforted. By then the rain was
picking up. Our umbrella was half
blown out, a mess of bent and broken
struts, but Mom, rallying,
pressed it into service. It kept
something between us and the weather.

# Government Cheese

# Government Cheese

Government cheese, Jack,
is a thing I hold no brief for.
Government cheese! Think I'm
too old to nose a whistle-pig in the corncrib?
I'm 84. I can't be had like some nickel-plated gimcrack. . . .
I'm the long ash that trails a spent cigarette. Don't
sleep with nobody, don't give a hoot
for baseball, the GDP. Don't play
Bingo nor Lotto nor this what-you-call
Paintball. . . . Got my arts down to a science:
steam my rice for fourteen minutes, including
boil the water, throw in some raisins. Religion
don't faze me. I'm no Baptist, but I'm
hard-shell and then some. . . . Tell you what:
I'd as soon cadge a ride on a cowcatcher as
cash a paycheck in one of these stagflationary shitstorms.
I'm a guy'd rather shear the spit curl from a sociopath than
tempt the Lord by hornswoggling a good Samaritan out of his
jumper cable, you follow me? Can I get an Amen?
*Alright, buster: Be that way!*

# U.S. 80 West, with the Barnstormers

The landscape stark, limb-strewn,
masticated. It's April 12, 2016. We
speed through Pennsylvania, whose
upcoming primary looks to figure big this
trash-talking, snake-handling, fear-mongering,
war-fraught election year. On the stereo: a
digitally mastered CD of a radio broadcast featuring
Ralph and Carter Stanley and the boys, singing from
another century, plugging Johnny's New & Used
Car Lot in Buckhannon, West Virginia, where the
cars are priced to move and Santa Claus
will be on hand till sundown and there's
coffee and donuts free for the taking, so
what the dickens 'you waitin' for? Limestoneville
flies by, a pastoral hallucination of
sheep, cows, haymows. "Tomorrow
I'll Be Gone," sings George Shuffler
(Carter drunk? hung over?), his boom-chuck
guitar a metronome, as a wood-smoked fiddle
shaves the top off the melody, then plunges
in a free fall of bluesy double-stops. He's
right, of course. It's mostly gone. Three
fast-food joints, then Paintball Free-For-All, then
Reptiland in Allenwood. Beyond town a
backlit cloud protrudes above a mountain.

Gas is $4.29 a gallon at the pump, but you'd
never guess it from the traffic. We cruise
through agribusiness vistas MapQuesting
the Williamsport Community Theater, venue
for a country music festival at which
the Barnstormers (no grassroots bandwagon
but a bluegrass band) will perform tonight.

There we'll pretend it's 1946, the
Crusades are history, ExxonMobil doesn't
own Congress, and the course of empire
has settled down for good, after two
millennia of westward migration, in
—fancy that?—our own backyard.

Where, though, *does* the westering end?
Or will the circle be unbroken in
the Thomas Cole "Course of Empire" sense?
It's hard enough to sort out our
lives' migrations, let alone the
nation's tail-devouring flight from
enlightenment, or these mind-numbing,
jump-cutting promotional trailers depicting
fast cars, big bucks, bare chests, guns,
conflagrations and bloodbaths that may
or may not, for all the head-cuffing
Surround Sound, be the Big Picture.

The broken line bends, grows iffy,
reappears where a canting barn yawns
and a big dog chases a small dog in
the shadow of a saltbox. We stop
for—say what?—a traffic light,
swaying at the crossroads of
Eat My Dust and Dust My Broom.
Four gas pumps and an oil drum oxidize.

I'm a sideman on this road trip, playing
breaks, fills, improvising. Bluegrass
is a heritage I filched because my native
Bronx burned down. These songs

of dislocation speak to me more than
any hymn or anthem. Tomorrow
we'll retrace the broken line to a
Code Orange city where prerecorded
subway announcements caution Watch
Your Step, a landscape of fire escapes
deadpans What Are You Nuts? and a
vanguard of pear trees steel themselves
to bust a move on Columbus Avenue.

# Trad Dance

Hands four. Can we please take
hands four? Gents opposite the
ladies . . . Or whoever is
dancing the role of the lady.
Or woman. The woman. If you're
dancing the part of the gent, turn
and face the, uh, your partner. . . .
But before we start: Look around
you, please. Someone has lost a
—Come again? I missed that—a
Zuni fetish. Anyone seen this chap's
Zuni fetish? Also, we're looking for
a—What?—a teal contact lens.
Check the soles of your shoes,
would you please? Or your feet,
if you're dancing barefoot, which,
jeez, everyone here seems to be . . .
The first dance will be in Becket
Formation. Each couple—What's
that? . . . Right. Who needs Becket
Formation? Instead, the band will
play a smooth jig, and we'll—Eh?
The band doesn't do jigs? Hey, no
problem . . . So the band's going to do
whatever it's going to do, and, dancers,
you're going to, uh, freestyle for ten
minutes. King Tut, Funky Penguin,
whatever. After that, the band's going
to play a reel—any two-part reel:
Northern, Southern, Western, North-
by-Northwestern. . . . Actually, any
tune with a beat is fine: J. Lo?
Arctic Monkeys? Say what? Hey,

no problem, whatever sounds
good on the theremin. Then we'll, uh,
take a break and announce the winner
of the door prize, which this week is a
pair of buckwheat-hull ear muffs and a
free pass to next week's dance, but first,
Look around you, please: Someone's
lost a pewter nipple ring. . . .

# Exploding Toads?

Needing a break from the
*New York Times,* CNN and
the new millennium, in which
atrocities multiply and anxious
regimes bulk up on nuclear
technology or revert to Cold
War neuroses, I pick up *The
National Mirror,* whose
banner headline reads:
*Exploding Toads!*
                    "This
weekend as day-trippers from
Hamburg, Germany, arrived at
a popular picnic spot north
of the city, they encountered
a scene of grotesque carnage.
The blown-apart carcasses
of thousands of cane toads
lay strewn, piecemeal, on the
grass and along the banks of
a pristine lake."
                Tabloid hoax?
Industrial pollutants—cocktails
of toxic chemicals leaching
into the soil? Something
to do with microbes?
terrorists? germ
warfare (imagination
ever the blowpipe)?
                    No:
The toads, it says, were
frightened to death by
large flocks of crows—
birds whose population,

a German biologist notes,
has surged in recent years.
"The toad's reflex, when
danger menaces, is to
take in air, expanding
to nearly four times its
ordinary size. The
spectacle scares away
many predators." But
the crows weren't fazed.
And so, "The toads'
panic buttons became
stuck on 'bloat.'" They
scared themselves to pieces.

# Popular Cetology

Gingerly, he stroked the Naugahyde flank.
Here was intelligence, humor, echolocation—
an acoustic panel in the lower jaw capable of pinpointing
        a cough drop in a coral reef. . . . Cripes,
what lines! If a Lamborghini were amphibious . . .

No one ever saw Sandy with another dolphin.
Cavorting off San Salvador, he dogged the divers,
furtively, at first; then cannily; then rambunctious as a pup,
nuzzling the wet-suited bimbos with his sleek rostrum.

                \*

Tuna expeditions came and went.
"I love all animals," said Gus, spitting into an oil drum.
His stubby fingers plucked a fiddler crab from a bucket
as porpoises thwacked the smack's prow. "Take these boogers . . ."

Is the navy turning dolphins into kamikazes?
Gus scoffed at the allegation.
"They're like wise men in dolphin suits," added Lenny, the winch
        hand. "They're *akamai*—
smart, really together. Too hip to stooge for the admiral."

                \*

Fingering the appropriate lever, Earl asked the animal, "Is there
        anything out there?"
Nudging a red ball meant yes.
Over a background chorus of snapping shrimp came the staccato
        click.
"Boy, was *he* training *me!*"

Sandy vanished as suddenly as he had appeared.
Each night brought blankets of crustaceans, schools of smelts.
Tucuxi, Bottlenose, Boutu, Ganges Susu—these are some
    extraordinary species of porpoise,
though for sheer alien beauty, nothing outstrips the fiberglass hide
    of Grampus Griceus.

# "Chess Robot Grabs and Breaks Boy's Finger"

AI is *we,* its engineers—
no more or less—all of us
artificially intelligent at best
(native smarts turbocharged
by culture, history). It dazzles,
fabricates, drives profits,
games options, outperforms—
and breaks fingers. "The
7-year-old, overenthusiastic,
moved his rook too quickly."
Well, *exactly!* This game we're
rushing into, this algorithmic
gambit, is unpredictable and
for keeps. *Check, mate!*

# Thank You for Your Patience

Attention passengers: The
Long Island Railroad apologizes
for this delay, caused by a
deranged individual throwing
himself on the tracks. We
hope to be moving shortly.

# Complimentary Tool

To receive my free, collapsible, aluminum-and-nickel-plated pocket tool, I need only mail in two box tops from my favorite lending institution, subscribe to one of 300 professional journals or trade magazines *(Popular Mycology? Camshaft and Piston?)* or give my social security or employee identification number to any three Third-World countries. Alternatively, I can elect to respond to a six-page questionnaire exploring my personal experience with a variety of skin diseases or liposuction procedures, or merely verify the spelling of my name, my mother's maiden name and the e-mail addresses of six female friends or dependents, or switch my long-distance service to any one of several fiber-optic startups currently negotiating to acquire gateway services and operating rights throughout the Northeast. Nothing could be easier, says the lime-scented blowout folded into my February gas & electric bill, than to receive my own monogrammed, rust-resistant, $39.95-value tool by purchasing any of several warrantied home appliances, vacation cruise packages or samples of adult educational software. A brochure photo shows a microwave shaving-cream dispenser, a pair of 72-inch walnut speaker cabinets, a couple playing water volleyball in a resort swimming pool, laughing uncontrollably beneath a patent-leather sky.

# Reading the News Online

Needing a break from editing copy, I
click on the news, scan the leading
stories (suicide bombing, mudslide,
arson, kidnapping, prisoner abuse),
then click on BACK. But the
soccer ball is spinning, spinning; the
old screen won't reconstitute itself.

# To the Kansas Board of Education

Forget the science. I'm walking in the park,
late afternoon, August. A thwack. A buzz.
A blur of insects sizzles to the ground.
The aftermath is quiet, businesslike:
The hornet lugs the thumb-sized, ashen moth
across the path to the foot of a sycamore
and up the mottled trunk some 20 feet,
then flies away, the stung, immobilized
moth clutched to its abdomen, enslaved—
as it will remain for weeks, while the wasp
lays its brood of eggs and the hatchling larvae
feed on the flesh of the paralytic moth,
instinctively avoiding vital organs.
My point? Assume intelligent design.
What must your children think of such a god?

# Donut Shop

Young night clerk tidies
up to a boom-box's lilt:
the chanted Koran.

# Pioneering the New Frontier

The die was cast, and now, you joked, the cast
must die so the credits could roll. Gloved fingers
entwined, we watched as they cut the cable. (So
much for fond leave-takings; cue the shot
of heavenly bodies pirouetting in the distance.)
All night we surfed the harvest moon's penumbra,
the booster rockets shucked like manzanita
seed pods in a late-September heat wave.

By twenty-four-hundred every affective
impulse had been stanched. Memory
was screening in black and white. Language
was a compromised code in rewrite. You
flicked your index absently at the remote
and said that we had done it after all.

Shadow

# Riverside Park: September

It happens gradually, but you
notice it with a start: the trees'
noonday shadows all but own
the promenade, though their leaves
remain green, intact. . . . It's just
a trick of light, the tilt of earth's
axis as it plies its orbit, but
the message is clear: the game is on.

# Blood Moon

*September 27, 2015*

We were out for blood:
the spectacle of a
bland, opalescent face
reduced to a split lip.
When a cloud got between
us and the bloodletting, we
cursed the obtrusive ref, the
invisible handler's styptic.
In the wee hours, the champ
reappeared—composed,
lucid, nonchalant. WTF?
We stalked off to sleep, eyes
red around the rims, burning.

# Sin-Eater

*Sin-eaters risked their souls to
soak up the misdeeds of the dead.*
—Wikipedia

Because I'm a wretch, they
employ me, offer me
bread, ale, a
place at the fire. The
corpse lies on its
bier. I'm
eating his sins (some
blackberry-sweet, most
like rancid pork) so
he won't have to
walk the earth, a
haggard shade. I'll
get what he's got
coming, drag my
chains a little
longer. Not
much of a deal, yet
a reprieve for us both.

# Whodunit

W.H. Auden famously surmised
the function of the whodunit: to free
*the rest of us* from blame. The tale's devised
to bring to light the murderer whose spree
has flummoxed Scotland Yard, the FBI—
thereby exculpating you and me.
But Auden's insight begs the question why
—model citizens though we may be—
we inwardly should yearn to be absolved:
What guilt so implicates us that we lie
abed speed-reading till the crime is solved?
What have we done that we cannot justify
save at the expense of the butler or his cohort?
What underlies this thinking man's blood sport?

# Persona Non Grata

Let's get something straight: I'm
the persona here. *I'm* the one
talking to you—not that other one,
the one who put me here, whose
experience isn't mine, though I'm
not above siphoning off some of it
for my own purposes. If I tell you
about, oh, day breaking on purple
loosestrife, that's me, the speaker,
appreciating what the damn things
look like early in the morning—*me,*
not the other one. That loafer
hasn't been awake at sunup for
thirty years and doesn't know one
plant from another. He might have
driven through Vermont once and
seen them along the median, so
many night lights left on. Or not.
Why get into supposition? Point is,
your business isn't with him, it's with
me, your persona. Jeez, I shouldn't
have to tell you this. But I
know the other guy and get
feedback from time to time.
Some of it really ticks me off.

# Sagaponack

The sea usurped the beach. Raw wind
swept monarchs from the briny grass.
Crepe paper wings caught fire en masse,
the lesser royalty drowning.

We were happy, we told ourselves, in Sagaponack.
Spuds for breakfast, butternut squash for lunch.
But the halcyon rumbled. October's sun
drove the Dutch elm's shadow across the door.

Slate waves pummeled the southern shore.
Nimbuses braised in tropical flues blew
north, raining hailstones as the Queen Anne's lace crumbled.
So much contended. So little was resolved.

In summer the socialites alight.
It's famous for its lionized avant-garde.

# From between Parked Cars

The cyclist looked left
through the windshield of a van
but never saw the van

that struck him, his bike
a bottle cap popped, spinning
skyward, then meeting

the tabletop of
asphalt street. There wasn't the
shadow of a doubt.

# Lost Edge

When I was young, my poems had
edge—a high-roller's attitude toward
language, a mannered
incoherence to die for. I
launched them like spitballs at the
wiggier journals.
Some of them stuck.

\*

What were they like? Oh,
full of beans: disjunctions,
expostulations, images cribbed from
Trakl, de Chirico—plus a lot of rubbish
imbibed from the mimeographed
rants of local maniacs. I was all about
voice. My voice, I called this heist.

\*

These days, I've lost my edge. I don't
believe in voice. I stand aside,
let each poem speak for itself.
Dumb as a parent, I try to supply
structure, a reality check, tough love—
a chance for a spit-curled, wise-ass
poem to make something of itself.

# Math for Poets

Two of the problems, he noticed, featured a cosine motif. In a third, two trains had left a station, traveling at different speeds and going in different directions. Hmm. The gesture of narrative but an elliptical one, certain details erased, sort of a Robbe-Grillet affair . . . No doubt "x" equaled something, but why indulge in supposition? Surely an informing subtext would emerge with successive readings. . . . In this one, the graph of a function was approaching its asymptote. The way his romances never did. They tended to be intersecting lines— meet and get gone, two ships crashing in the night, two trains stoked and coupling, then uncoupling, leaving the station, abscissa this way, ordinate that. . . . *Is the function hyperbolic?* Hell, he supposed so, but don't we all exaggerate a bit where the emotions are concerned? Not that they were, in his case— he hoped he was way past *that*. But, well, aren't they almost always? Even in the most objective accounts? How many pages does Robbe-Grillet expend depicting a smooshed centipede in *Jealousy?* Isn't absence a shadowy form of presence? D.S. had once asked, apropos of the riptide lusts so conspicuously missing from his college poems on Spinoza. . . . The next problem featured terms that could only be called impacted: polynomial train wrecks, really. Whoever penned this equation needed to sit down and read Ernest Fenollosa's essay on the Chinese written character, whose pictographic elegance—each one a stick-figure video, a cave painting— dramatizes "less is more." Unless the sclerotic style— parenthetical this, radical-encrusted that—was the point? He had been, once, to the Quaker graveyard on Nantucket memorialized in *Lord Weary's Castle* (apropos of a sclerotic style that *was* the point, line after hermetic line). He imagined it now, beset by a December nor'easter: blue-black sky, sleet strafing expressionistically askew headstones. . . . The next problem announced itself with a regal imperative—a voice that, he was coming to see, pervaded Cartesian geometry: *Given a circle with radius "r," let the square of "r" be one of the nonparallel sides of an isosceles trapezoid."* Yes, SIR! Whatever you say, Daryl. Anything else you'd like me to assume? Some servile position, perhaps? You're a surd, Daryl; a geometric stolid, an extraneous root, a Boolean mooncalf, a

*Time's up. Pass them forward.*

Say what? I'm, uh, not quite ready to share this effort with the class just yet. . . .

# Tumbleweed Mischief

*after James Tate*

Tumbleweed mischief ensconces the rotunda. Sometimes
I'm a hurt newt, a burnt scarab, a slipshod yawn, a
font of feckless paterfamilias. Broken
footstools litter my landscape, and no stone
goes unburned out there where caimans thunder and
hummingbirds levitate above a trickling effluent.
This is how it was twelve miles from Norman:
Snoods roosting as the crow flies; old
scarves mottled with snide fandangos. . . .
Nothing *reciprocates* anymore. We yearn, swoon,
sulk like downsized straw bosses—to no avail. (This
lout with the bawdily furnished face is proficient at a
certain type of Zen codicil that's been cropping up in
certain sleepy border towns, rank as maize in a Mayan
dig, vaulted corncribs in a civet's shirtsleeve. . . .) Well,
I'll be switched: Whose full-grown spawn is this
loitering in the shadow of the arboretum?
Humor me: Close your eye and
count to ten. Can't you just
see yesterday's tonnage evolve in
serendipitous emoluments? Still,
it pays to crack the whip, to
ferret out the dross, cinch the saddle, tighten the
drumhead, prune the dead wood, burn the empty receptacles.
Especially after one of these Oklahoma cloudbursts.

# Phatic

> *Dr. [Robin] Dunbar notes that social animals like monkeys spend an inordinate amount of time grooming one another. The purpose is not just to remove fleas but also to cement social relationships. But as the size of a group increases, there is not time for an individual to groom everyone.*
>
> *Language evolved, Dr. Dunbar believes, as a better way of gluing a larger community together.*
> —New York Times, July 15, 2003

This kind of speech has nothing much to say
—and yet too much. Oblivious to time,
it natters, its nonverbal paradigm
the chase-and-race, perhaps, of dogs at play;
chimps' grooming tête-a-têtes: a sublime
social ritual; a stroke-and-joke exchange
of scolding, flirting, bantering; a range
of "What's up? / Say what?" gestures read as rhyme
is processed when we read a poem. How strange
that we, whose feelings bruise so easily;
whose fondest relationships are wont to fray
over felt slights; who become at times deranged
by misprisions, misperceptions, fumbled cues,
should trust to small talk for such vital news.

## "Dig Deep!"

says the runner's T-
shirt. I'm a poet, not a
runner. But I try.


The runner makes the
cinders fly, while I ply foot
after plodding foot.


Head down, the runner
guts it out, breaks the tape. I'm
my own finish line.


I finish a line,
pen poised above spiral pad,
a ballpoint drill bit.


Sure, you fear you'll run
out of will, hit a wall. That's
partly why you drill.


Then there's the fear of
breaking through . . . To what? What
hibernating self?


Beyond fear, failure
and the fear of failure—the
geode of the poem.

# Fridge

### 1

I would open the door compulsively,
stare inside as if it were a TV, never
mind that I lived on bananas and rice
crackers and cared for little else. It was
the sense of bounty going forward, the way
the boxed light lured and hypnotized me.

### 2

Decades later, my finicky appetite
was ancient history, but my diet had
become restricted. I'd developed
health issues. Nights when I couldn't
sleep, I'd open the door a crack, practice
looking past the wedge of light.

### 3

Last time the bulb blew, the hardware
store had stopped carrying the model
and the company that made the fridge
had gone under. It's a forlorn thing, an
unlit fridge. Still works, though. I'm
getting used to the unwonted dark.

# Shard

Curbside, where the pocked tarmac dips
in the shadow of the law school overpass,
something glistens: a shard of red glass.
I pick it up, hold it by its tips:
*'63—the Nocturnal Mammals House,*
*the Bronx Zoo. A transistor radio plays*
*("O, Denise, ooby-doo . . .") as red eyes blaze*
*behind glass. Lemurs swoop. An albino mouse—*
*infrared ghost—noses wood chips. I*
*snake an arm around Alana's back;*
*we French-kiss in the artificial night. . . .*
Damn! I've cut myself. . . . Sallow light
glares. Heat rises, rippling, from the black-
top. Din of traffic. The years whiz by.

# Van Cortlandt Park: November

Fall spreads itself thick here:
the cross-country trail's leaf-
cluttered path; the flanking trees
and their shadows—obtuse
angles set off by spangled
sunlight, pointillist foliage.

I walk this two-and-a-half-mile
course, remembering: the busting
hump, the fail-fail-succeed; leaf
storms of love, jealousy, want. . . .
The trail ascends, spotlit by
shafts of mote-churning light.

To my left, a deer and buck
accompany me. They move in
tandem with each other, keeping
pace with me for a stone's throw,
then freeze, listening. I continue on
past a gorge, a brake of sumac, a

stand of woods where bare limbs
predominate, then lose my footing;
sprawl, open my eyes, face full of
leaves and cinders. I'm not hurt.
But where's my second wind?
*Can I get a second wind, please?*

Down on the flats, afternoon
steeps. The gusts, unbuffered,
make walking a chore, but late
light floods the acres of grass.
In my racing days, I'd be kicking
hard now, going for broke. . . .

# Thanksgiving, 2016

No traffic; no one stirring on the street.
A quiet like that, perhaps, of the earliest
Puritan Thanksgiving, 1637
(the previous night's labors in the Lord's
vineyard having prospered: the Pequot
village torched, Pequots incinerated).
I walk south through Central Park. A hawk
circles above Great Lawn, the foliage
brilliantly stupefied in the absence of wind.
The election's over, and we've screwed the pooch,
the beyond-the-pale male candidate gone
from unelectable to ineluctable.
That's his building—a gilded middle finger
protruding above the mid-Manhattan skyline. . . .

Blame Russia's campaign cyber-sabotage,
the Electoral College's back-door-oiling hocus,
mainstream media's mesmerized reporting
of tweeted claptrap, the alt-right media's
alchemy of falsehood into fact,
the FBI chief's Halloween intervention
head-cuffing the undecideds, the relocated
polling places—some of them "monitored."
But don't forget the blame that *we've* incurred:
the quietly misogynistic votes;
the uncast votes and statement-making votes;
the screw-you votes—game but blindly angry—
cast by left-behinds who thought the ranting
plutocrat would somehow have their backs. . . .

When Arthur Dimmesdale, in *The Scarlet Letter,*
delivers his Election Day address,
it concerns not politics, but the prospect
of his charges' being saved; of God's "elect"

staying the course; of John Winthrop's City
on a Hill (as Winthrop had imagined
the still-unfounded Boston settlement's
legacy from the deck of the *Arbella*)
being perfected in a wilderness.
His sermon over, Dimmesdale bares his chest.
What his parishioners see, or think they see, there
is an "A": *Adulterer? Angel? America?*
Hawthorne keeps his finger off the scale—
just winks and floats the possibilities.

*Who are we?* What do we—won't we—stand for?
We chose the chest-thumper—the swinging dick;
the waterboarder, P.O.W.-mocker,
race-baiter, wall-builder, war-hawk, business fraud;
the fact-trasher, press-basher, liar, pussy-grabber. . . .
We chose a demagogue who urged supporters
to punch out hecklers; "Second Amendment folks"
to muster up in the event his bid should fail. . . .
I'm looking for a silver lining to this long
shadow darkening the park; a fall
epiphany; a morsel of black humor—
something to be grateful for, as bigots,
troglodytes and bottom-feeders rise
like scum to the surface of the melting pot.

# Limbo of Lost Gloves (A Double Feature)

Like severed hands, they litter the ground.
Tan leather, black suede; dark brown cotton,
a triangle of red interior visible. And now
a homeless man wearing one of my own
lost gloves crouches before me in the
shadow of an overpass. . . .

I rise from my plush folding seat; take
half a dozen steps up the aisle, pondering
the opaque dream's missing denouement.
The usher pulls me aside and clues me in.
Turning off his flashlight, he informs me
that I've actually been dreaming about lost
*loves,* not gloves. . . . (These do indeed
litter the landscape: hands I won't hold
again, each picked up by some other guy—
homeless, perhaps, as I am in the larger
sense, aging bachelor that I've become;
and whom I can't bring myself, out of a
mix of pity, fear and pride, to challenge.)

I thank him, compliment him on his acuity,
exit the theater and wake up, exhausted.

# Some Personas

'Thing is, with an ax to grind and
a mouth that won't take no for an
answer, he's gonna be a player, you
follow me? Never mind his glass
jaw, the guy is stoked; he's gonna
lead with his chin, you know? Some
personas are like that: You can't
tell them nothing. *Nothing.* And you
know what? Some of them make it
work for them. I seen one once,
came out of the gate flapping his
lips like one of these what-you-call
terrarium fish, the hell with every other
voice in the on-deck circle. Sure, he
gets taken down a peg or three, has to
pipe down, nurse his pride for a while.
You think that stops him? Just listen:
He's ranting like a maniac right now,
never mind the rest of us bums who
sometimes, just sometimes,
might if you don't mind like to
interject a word in edgewise.
You tell me, Jack: What, are we
dirt? What are we, garbage?!

# What She Notices

*for my sister, Barbara Daniel*

Each June her fingernails begin to grow
like gangbusters, she says. And when she takes
a vitamin C supplement, no toenail breaks,
grows brittle, splits, curls or fails to show
a pale moon just below the cuticle,
she says. She keys in to such things;
registers that one of the draw-drapes' rings
has jumped the track; spots the *Dispatch* article
on the hometown kid whose science project won
a national award; twigs to the common parlance
for all the local plants and prepared foods;
and patters like Linnaeus in the woods,
marking Virginia creeper at a glance
and dwarf Nandina in a patch of sun.

# Autumn Haiku

Cliff Notes version: The
black locust's gold upstages
summer's green machine.


Night's gambit: the moon—
a blood orange, hovering;
a gauntlet thrown down.


October's colors
steep: orange pekoe, cut black
pekoe, Darjeeling.


A gale lacquers the
black locusts' trunks, the sidewalk's
chrome-mango collage.


Late-November wind
rattles the turkey oak's dry
boughs: a smoker's cough.


Twenty-one degrees.
The spirit breath takes leave, flies
south for the winter.

# Cold Comfort

The sycamores' gargantuan shadows flung
across sidewalks treacherous with sleet and snow;
the early evening traffic—stop-and-go
on the West Side Highway, where a throng
of merging cars is at a standstill . . . No
use dreaming of greener seasons, days
of biking to work, weekends of soaking up rays
in the park. Now it's wool pullovers, cups of joe,
the radio tuned to the weather channel, heat
hissing and clanking in radiators and pipes.
Time to savor buttermilk scones, sweet-
meats oven-hot from the pastry shop;
tangerines, pomegranates, sugar beets—
winter's booby prize, a bumper crop.

# Health Salad

I shop because your health is poor, and I'm
sweating bullets. Scores of clementines,
each one the size of an endometrial tumor,
spread themselves across an inclined plane.
I grab one, palpate it, force myself to focus
long enough to process what the doctor said:
"Thirty percent chance of recurrence if we go
the chemo-radiation route. . . ." And yet,
how not to? Now one hand is holding kiwis
I've never seen before. My shopping cart
is filling up with star fruit, apricots,
mangos, papayas, blackberries, ugli fruit. . . .
I speed-dial: "Is there something nice you'd like?
Come again? Sure thing." A box of raisins d'être.

# Chestnuts, Roasting

Christmas songs monopolized the air waves.
Brightly scarved, we traded season's greetings,
tossed back flutes of—*ahem*— "holiday cheer."
(The thing, back then, was never to let on.)

Brightly scarved, we traded season's greetings.
But the carols lied; joy proved elusive.
The thing, of course, was never to let on.
(In a pinch, one might confess to "feeling blue.")

The carols lied. Joy proved elusive.
Daytime came up short; the nights were—silent.
In a pinch, one might confess to "feeling blue"
like Elvis, when he blu-blu-blu-ed "Blue Christmas."

Daytime came up short; the nights were—silent.
So we played the radio, tra-la-la-ed the hits
like Elvis, when he blu-blu-blu-ed "Blue Christmas"
in the movies. (That's where top-draw pop stars went—

having paid the radio jockeys to play their hits—
to make back what the record companies stole.)
The movies: That's where choused pop singers went.
And we went too, having outgrown Christmas pageants.

To make back what the record companies stole,
pop singers went to Hollywood—or Vegas.
And we went too, having outgrown Christmas pageants
and realized the true meaning of Christmas.

We dreamt Hollywood, got away to Vegas!
And holiday songs monopolized the airwaves.
Realizing the true meaning of Christmas,
we tossed back flutes of cheer and hit the tables.

# The Human Balcony

No: That's an "*n*," not an "*m.*"
Again I've misread the name of the
Chinese restaurant. What's up with that?

*

Hoist onto my father's shoulders in the
morning light of the housing project—
swept up from the realm of 3-year-old
fecklessness into that of adult omnipotence—
I'm riding the camel-like rhythms of his
stride, looking down at all that ordinarily
towers over and intimidates: the
garbage men emptying cans of ash, the
cans of ash, the T-shirted teen, portable
radio blaring into his pompadour.

*

But hovering behind this association is
another: that of dying as being ushered
into the balcony of a theater—dark, tucked
away, cordoned off—a sullen tier where
the dead smoke and stare, inconspicuous
to the living, who are absorbed in the
show they're watching, the hand they're
holding, the creature from the tarn that
looms above an ashen face, frightening
and sexy. . . . The dead have seen this flick.
Their sweet and sour scorn hangs in the air
like cigarette smoke in the projector's beam
as the credits roll and the house lights rouse
dazed patrons from plush orchestra seats.

# Shadow

The harried squirrel bobs and weaves for dear
life on the crab apple's stunted trunk. Below,
a raptor twice the size of a carrion crow
—brindled feathers: goshawk?—denied a clear
flight line, hunches, motionless, and glares
at the dodgy animal whose neck he'd break,
whose palpitating shanks he'd like to take
to a remote limb for his morning fare.
I've been where that squirrel is; have stared
a semiautomatic in the eye.
I remember each propitiatory lie,
each vow I made to a God who isn't there,
if only He would save my sorry ass. . . .
The hawk desists. Its shadow rakes the grass.

# About the Author

Bill Christophersen grew up in the Bronx and studied poetry at Columbia University, where he received a doctorate in American literature. He is the author of five previous poetry collections—*Two Men Fighting in a Landscape, The Dicer's Cup, Tableau with Crash Helmet, Where Truth Lies,* and *Why the Gods Don't Get It*—as well as two literary studies, *The Apparition in the Glass: Charles Brockden Brown's American Gothic* and *Resurrecting Leather-Stocking: Pathfinding in Jacksonian America*.

His book reviews and critical essays have appeared in *Newsweek, Poetry, The New Leader, The New York Times Book Review,* and *The American Book Review*. His poems have won prizes from *Kansas Quarterly, Rhino* and *The Robinson Jeffers Tor House Foundation* and have been nominated for a Pushcart Prize. He lives in New York and plays traditional fiddle.

www.ingramcontent.com/pod-product-compliance
Lightning Source LLC
Chambersburg PA
CBHW072049160426
43197CB00014B/2693